HOW TO ANALYZE PEOPLE

2

How to Analyze People

How to Read Body Language, Behavior, Social Cues, and Employ Powerful Psychological Tactics to Gain Deep Insights into Those around You

*

Pascal Langdon

4

Legal Notice

Copyright (c) 2019 Pascal Langdon.

All rights are reserved. No portion of this book may be reproduced or duplicated using any form whether mechanical, electronic, or otherwise. No portion of this book may be transmitted, stored in a retrieval database, or otherwise made available in any manner whether public or private unless specific permission is granted by the publisher.

This book does not offer advice, but merely provides information. The author offers no advice whether medical, financial, legal, or otherwise, nor does the author encourage any person to pursue any specific course of action discussed in this book. This book is not a substitute for professional advice. The reader accepts complete and sole responsibility for the manner in which this book and its contents are used. The publisher and the author will not be held liable for any damages caused.

Contents

Introduction 8

The Importance of Being Able To Read People 9

Common Myths About Body Language 15

Basic Strategy for Analyzing People 24

How to Analyze Facial Expressions 31

How to Analyze People Based on How They Talk 45

How to Analyze People in a Romantic Setting 73

Advanced Strategies for Analyzing People: Cold Reading 84

Final Thoughts: Can You Really Fake Body Language? 92

INTRODUCTION

Your ability to read other people will significantly affect how you deal with them. It's a technique often used by agencies like the FBI with the aim of predicting or determining an individual's thoughts and intentions based on their facial expression, speech, and body language. You don't have to be a CIA or FBI agent, though, to be able to learn how to analyze people. There are ways for you to find out what other people are thinking and feeling just by observing some of their gestures and mannerisms, and that's what this book aims to discuss.

Being able to read people has more to do with simply being able to interpret a person's body language. And anyone can have this ability. The only thing that's required is for one to recognize what to look for. This includes a person's facial expression, tone of voice, posture, hand gestures, and other physical movements.

THE IMPORTANCE OF BEING ABLE TO READ PEOPLE

Knowing how to analyze people's behaviors can have a significant impact on every aspect of your life. You may think that with the advent of modern technology communication has never been as convenient. After all, we now have the ability to send countless text messages and electronic mails every minute. Nevertheless, despite the fact that we as humans are advancing in technology, it's safe to say that this generation is the worse when it comes to reading people. We are connected to the internet 24 hours a day, 7 days a week, and yet we have never been as disconnected from each other. And that's the reason we are missing a lot in our lives.

According to studies, you can predict the outcome of a negotiation simply by reading and interpreting the body language of the people involved. The reason is that words aren't the only thing that account for the effectiveness of communication, and the only way for one to gain advantageous ground is by paying attention to things like facial expression, tone of voice, and body language. While having the ability to read people can have several benefits, it's not about mind reading, though. Reading and analyzing people is about observing and discerning another person, and making adjustments based on your interpretation so that you can communicate better with them. But why is having this ability so important?

For one, we get to deal with people of different personality types every day of our lives, and we need to be familiar which one has this or that personality type. This allows us to be able to better deal with them.

AT HOME

If you're married with kids, it's crucial that you are able to recognize what's going on in the minds and emotions of your loved ones if you are to connect with them in a more intimate manner. When it comes to your partner, for instance, it's important that you can read what's on their mind just through the tone of their voice. We want know that we are heard by our partners, and they feel the same way, too. They want to know that you understand what they're going through, but sometimes, they can't say it directly through words. It's during such crucial moments that they need you to read their thoughts and emotions even without them having to say a word.

The same is true with young people, especially teenagers. Teenagers are in a season of their lives when all they want is to be heard and understood. They are in a way confused, and the last thing they want is you not being able to perceive their real thoughts and feelings. However, if you know how to read them even if they won't tell you what they actually think and feel, you'll be able to come up with better strategies of communicating with them without them feeling that you're a dictator.

IN THE WORKPLACE

If having the ability to read other people is important inside the home, having the same ability is more crucial in the workplace. It's easy to recognize what a family member is thinking or feeling since you're with them all the time and are familiar with their ways. It's a different story, though, in the workplace. There, you encounter a myriad of people coming from different backgrounds (and possibly, culture), and missing social cues is more probable.

Knowing how to analyze your colleague's personalities is crucial because it determines how effective you are in working with them and vice versa. Aside from your own personality, you also need to understand the personality of people you're working with because it affects the way they act and make decisions. When you're good at reading people at work, may it be your co-workers or your seniors, it will be easier for you to deal with them since you can adjust your behavior and your relationship with them. It will also help you determine which persons are easy to work with and which ones you should be more patient with.

IN SOCIAL GATHERINGS

Being able to read people in a social context is necessary for humans to blend, which is why children are taught to begin doing it at an incredibly young age. Of course, not all of us grow up to be adept when it comes to recognizing social cues, but we all know how critical such a skill is, especially when you're in social gatherings. The main difference of social gatherings from home and work is that, here, you meet people you may have only met for the first time. And while you're not out there to impress people, it's still important for you to establish rapport, and one way to do that is by knowing how to read people and adapt to the situation.

When you're in a party, for instance, and are looking for opportunities to get to know people of the opposite sex, knowing how to read body language will give you an idea who's into you and who's not. The amount of space a person gives you, eye contact, mannerisms, and other gestures will tell you whether a person is enjoying the time with you or is anxious to leave the conversation.

That said, the benefits of knowing how to read people goes beyond the family setting, but extends to the workplace and social settings. When you understand the rules of analyzing people just by observing how they behave, you can gain an advantage, and that advantage can determine your chance for career advancement, for finding a suitable partner in life, and for building stronger relationships with people around you.

COMMON MYTHS ABOUT BODY LANGUAGE

There is no denying that most body language is universal. A smile, for example, is a smile regardless of which part of the world you are from. However, before we proceed, you need to understand that interpretations of body language are complicated by several factors, including culture, social dynamics, personal habits, and certain circumstances. So, when we say that this body language can be interpreted as this or that, you also need to understand that it's not one-hundred percent accurate at all times.

Becoming an expert in body language is not simply about recognizing gestures and facial expressions; it's mostly about understanding context. The same facial expression, gesture, or body language can have a hundred or even a thousand interpretations depending on the situation. That said, there are many commonly held beliefs about reading and interpreting body language that aren't precise, unless, of course, when they're applied in the right context. So what are these misconceptions about body language that we should be aware of? Here are a few of them:

Eye Movement Indicates Thought Patterns

It has long been thought that there's a direct link between eye movement and thought patterns[1], that you can predict what a person thinks and feels simply by looking them in the eye. Of course, there's some truth in this, but that's not always the case. In a series of studies done in 2012[2], it was discovered that no evidence supports the popular claim that you can tell whether a person is lying or not by observing the movement of their eyes. For instance, if a person is looking to the right, it's indicative of lying, and if the person is looking up to the left, it means they're telling the truth. The study found that this isn't always the case.

LIARS DON'T MAKE EYE CONTACT

While it would seem to make sense for people hiding something to avoid eye contact, it doesn't happen all the time. It's a long-held belief that people who are lying will have their eyes shift to avoid eye contact, but this is not the case with habitual or pathological liars. Pathological liars

---

[1]

https://www.theguardian.com/science/neurophilosophy/2015/jun/02/how-your-eyes-betray-your-thoughts

[2]

https://journals.plos.org/plosone/article?id=10.1371/journal.pone.0040259

excel at making eye contact and appearing very sincere. Also, avoiding eye contact can mean different things for different cultures. For instance, in Africa or Latin America, people have been taught from childhood never to look an authority in the eye, especially when they are being interrogated or criticized.

Moreover, lack of eye contact can also mean short attention span or even autistic spectrum disorder. Now, imagine a scenario where an office interrogates a person coming from the aforementioned cultural background, or is someone who has some sort of medical condition. The officer misinterpreting the lack of eye contact will surely have a lot of serious implications.

CROSSED ARMS INDICATE RESISTANCE

Most people consider the folding of arms as a rude gesture, taking it as a sign that the person crossing their arms lack openness. Nothing could be further from the truth, however. While the folding of arms could seem to be an expression of hostility and defensiveness, it's not the case all the time. People fold their arms for such reasons, but that depends on the situation.

If you're in a room and sees a person crossing their arms, it doesn't necessarily mean that they are skeptical toward what you're saying. Examine the situation first, because it could also mean that the chair they're sitting on doesn't have an arm support. It could also mean that the person has low tolerance to the cold and the room's AC is in full blast.

Finally, it could mean that the person is concentrating. In a study published in 2007 in the European Journal of Social Psychology [3], researchers found that that crossing of arms led to greater concentration and persistence when the person is involved in solving a problem. So, the next time you notice someone crossing their arms while you're making a presentation, avoid making the conclusion that they don't want to listen to you. On the contrary, they may be thinking deeply about what you're saying. Or, perhaps the AC is just too strong.

MOVING THE HANDS WHEN TALKING IS A SIGN OF UNEASINESS

Excessive fidgeting is indeed a sign of easiness for some people. However, just because someone is

---

[3] https://onlinelibrary.wiley.com/doi/abs/10.1002/ejsp.444

using hand movements when communicating or "talking with their hands" doesn't mean they're uncomfortable. Communication is not limited to words, and there are times that hand movements are necessary to make a point. In the same manner, gestures help people track and interpret what you are trying to say. Moving your hands when you're talking also helps you concentrate. It improves the way you communicate as it helps improve verbal content and eliminate unnecessary fillers like 'umm' and 'uhh' when you're trying to convey something.

THE MORE EYE CONTACT, THE BETTER

It is often said in sales that the more eye contact you make, the more chances you have of closing a deal. In the same manner, you lose the effectivity of your message the moment you look away from your audience. This is a common held belief, but it is not always true. Strong eye contact is necessary when you're conveying a message or are trying to persuade someone, but in some cases, it could hurt your efficiency as a communicator. Just because a person looks you in the eye when talking doesn't always mean they're telling the truth or can be trusted.

Sometimes, looking a person straight in the eye for an extended period can send that person the wrong message. There are simply people who will get the wrong impression when if you look them in the eye for too long. In a study published in the journal Psychological Science[4], researchers have concluded that excessive eye contact can reduce persuasion. The study involved a group of people who listened to a speaker trying to persuade them about something. When the group maintained eye contact with the speaker, it led to less persuasion than when the group looked at the mouth of the speaker instead.

PUTTING HANDS BEHIND THE BACK DENOTES POWER

It's a common tip given by presentation coaches that holding the hands behind the back is a sign of power of dominance. There is no truth in this principle, however. In fact, research shows that this posture can indicate that a person cannot be trusted. Hiding your hands could mean that you're hiding something, and this causes people to become suspicious of you instead of them trusting you. Instead of placing your hands behind your

---

[4]

https://journals.sagepub.com/doi/abs/10.1177/0956797613491968

back to show that you're in charge, you might simply show the palm of your hands as it's a better way to build rapport.

Speaking of power, there's a similar pose called the "power pose." Some people refer to it as the "Superman" or the "Wonder Woman" pose, which, according to the TED talk speaker Amy Cuddy who popularized it, increases testosterone levels and lowers down cortisol levels. For a time, many people adopted the idea, with some even posting on the internet the impressive results they got when trying out the pose. However, just recently, Cuddy's co-researcher Dana Carney commented that it isn't one-hundred percent accurate. A study also found that power posing didn't have any effect on hormones and risk tolerance just as Cuddy said.[5]

---

[5]

https://journals.sagepub.com/doi/full/10.1177/09567976145 53946

FAST-TALKING PEOPLE CANNOT BE TRUSTED

Are you a fast-talker? If you are, you've probably been told at least once in your life that fast-talking people cannot be trusted. This belief came from the idea that most salesman talk really fast as a way to hide their true intention. However, just because a person talks fast doesn't necessarily mean they're out there to trick you. Studies say that people who talk fast simply do so because they use shorter pauses, and there's nothing wrong with it. On the other hand, people who talk slower take long pauses in between sentences. And if you come to think of it, there's a higher chance that these are the ones who may be trying to conceal something, because long pauses could mean (although not all the time) that they are trying to think hard about how they could fabricate details of their story.

FAKING BODY LANGUAGE IS WRONG

The words 'fake' and 'faking' seem to denote something negative, but that really depends on the context. When it comes to body language, faking could be a good thing, especially if your ultimate aim is to improve the overall quality of the way you communicate. Even in sales, there's nothing wrong with practicing how to fake a certain body language to get what you want. It may sound selfish, but organizations use it all the time and that's simply the truth in the world of sales.

BODY LANGUAGE ACCOUNTS FOR OVER 90% OF COMMUNICATION

This perhaps is the most commonly held belief regarding body language. It is widely quoted that non-verbal communication accounts for around 93% of communication, and verbal, only 7%. These numbers weren't random, though. They were the results of a study done in the 60s by Albert Mehrabian, currently Professor Emeritus of Psychology in UCLA. The findings of his study became popularly known as the "7%-38%-55% Rule" and have been misinterpreted through human communication seminars around the globe.

It's true that our body language plays a huge role in conveying our thoughts and emotions, though. However, it's improbable for you to convey information with 93% accuracy using only body language, unless you're doing sign language, of course.

BASIC STRATEGY FOR ANALYZING PEOPLE

There are different ways of analyzing people's behavior and interpreting their speech and actions to find out what they think and feel. You don't need to be a first-class interrogator, though, to find out what's going on in a person's head. After all, the signals are always there, and all you need to do is recognize what to look for.

CREATE A BASELINE

When it comes to reading people, one needs to have a baseline. By baseline, we mean the way a person acts under normal conditions. This can be a little tricky, though, because you'll need to get to know a person first to identify what their baseline is. One way you can do it is by sitting down with the person you want to be able to read better. It could be your spouse, your child, or even a friend -- the key is to find time to talk to them casually about topics that are non-threatening in nature, something that they wouldn't have any reason to lie about.

While doing so, take note of the way they behave, and give special attention to their eyes. Once you've established a baseline, that's the time you'll be able to better identify any unusual changes in their expression when they're hiding something.

LOOK FOR INCONSISTENCIES

Now that you have a baseline, it would be easier for you to read people by paying attention to inconsistencies. When a person is trying to hide their true intentions, there is usually a deviation from the baseline in terms of facial expression, tone of voice, and gestures. Some inconsistencies are more obvious than others, of course. For instance, it's not in our culture to shake our heads up and down when saying, "No."

What you need to be aware of are the inconsistencies that are a bit more vague. Let's say you have business partner who has a habit of clearing his throat when he's nervous. If one day you are doing business with that person and he suddenly clears his throat repeatedly, you should begin to think whether or not he's hiding something from you.

WATCH OUT FOR CLUSTERS OF GESTURES

There's a rule in reading body language called "The Rule of Four." This rule states that you can't accurately judge a person's intentions by attaching meaning to a single gesture. It calls for the reading of cues alongside other cues before coming up with conclusions. The cues here are referred to gesture clusters, a combination of movements or actions that gives a clearer meaning to what a person says or does.

It's not easy to find out what a person is thinking just by observing a single gesture, but when that gesture is accompanied by three or more other gestures, then interpreting the person's words or actions become easier. For instance, if you're having a conversation with someone and he begins scratching one of his eyes, the action wouldn't mean much by itself. But if the person is also turning the direction of his gaze, trying to avoid eye contact, and turns the direction of his feet toward the exit, then it's safe to say that the person isn't interested anymore and wants to leave.

COMPARE BEHAVIORS

Aside from simply looking for gesture clusters, you can also compare and contrast if you're not too sure. For instance, if you've noticed that someone's actions are a bit unusual when they're in your presence, observe whether they repeat the same behavior when they're with other people.

As the person interacts with a different group, check whether they're exhibiting the same facial expression and bodily gestures. Check their posture, too, and see if they're either more comfortable with the other group or not. If you notice that the gesture cluster has disappeared when they're with a different group and are more comfortable conversing with them, then there's a chance the person is hiding something from you.

NOTICE RECIPROCATION

Human beings have built-in mirror neurons in our brains that fire when we observe another person performing an action. It seems that we have been designed to read one another's bodily language. For instance, it's easy for us to smile when we see another person smile. A frown from another person, on the other hand, also seem to automatically activate our frown muscles. This principle can be very useful when trying to read another person.

When you see someone you like, for instance, your brain automatically sends signals to your body that make your facial muscles relax and increase the flow of blood to your lips. This also causes you to smile and project a positive behavior. If the other person reciprocates your actions, then it's clear that the other person likes you, too. On the other hand, if the other person doesn't seem to reciprocate your behavior, then there's a chance that he doesn't like you or isn't happy that you're around.

LISTEN TO THE VOICE

In a group, the most influential person is not always the one who claims to be the leader, but the one who's confident in his posture. And confident people usually have a strong voice. They also carry a huge smile on their face and a confident posture. If you're in a board meeting and are trying to suggest an idea to the group, your idea won't necessarily be heard just because you direct it to the "leader." What you would want to do instead is try to get the support of the most confident person in the table, the one with the strongest, most confident voice. If you can do this, you can expect your chances for success to dramatically increase.

OBSERVE HOW THE PERSON WALKS

A person's walking style says a lot about their personality. The speed and the motion may even change depending on the person's mood. Oftentimes, when a person lacks self-confidence, they will walk in a rather awkward way, usually lacking fluidity in their motion. Confident people walk in a manner that shows they know what they're doing and where they're headed. They usually walk briskly and with a forceful gait. These people are go-getters and can be an asset to an organization as they seem to value time.

And then there are those who seem to be sloppy, dragging their feet behind them as they walk. It's easy to be annoyed with such people since they seem to walk ever so slowly and seem to be unsure of where they are. However, if a person is walking in such a manner, it could be a sign that they simply need some sort of motivation. If you notice such traits in a colleague or a member of your organization, try helping building that person's confidence with a tap on the back or a heartfelt word of praise.

HOW TO ANALYZE FACIAL EXPRESSIONS

During a budget meeting with his vice president, Ryan noticed that his senior kept toying with her bracelet, sometimes shifting to toy with her necklace, too. Since Ryan knows that body language and facial expressions are indicators of what a person thinks and feels, he thought that the VP's mannerism was an indication that she was uncomfortable with the financial target Ryan was proposing. He also noticed that his senior's eyes seemed to convey that she's worried over the budget proposal. As a result, he kept asking her if she was fine with the budget target.

Despite the positive response of his VP during the meeting, Ryan wasn't convinced, and asked to meet with her on a different schedule for a follow-up meeting. Later on, he realized that he read the VP wrong and that he just wasted his time and hers for a meeting that wasn't necessary. Ryan's story is fictional, but it reminds us how misleading body language and facial expression can be. And if you're not trained at reading people, you might end up in embarrassing situations similar to what Ryan got involved in.

But that's not the only reason you need to learn how to read facial expressions. Experts say that when you're accurate at interpreting nonverbal communications, particularly facial expressions, you have a higher chance of becoming an effective leader. Being able to read facial expressions is an especially useful skill if you're a business executive, because oftentimes, people don't say what they think when they're in business settings.

On the other hand, if you could easily recognize how emotions manifest on the face, you'd be able to make decisions more quickly. For instance, when you notice that someone in a meeting is starting to get angry, you can immediately say or do something to help diffuse that anger. You'd also be able to recognize when people are trying to hide emotions such as fear, disgust, or even contempt. In the end, your ability to read people's facial expressions and interpret them will better equip you at handling sensitive or crucial situations during office or business meetings.

This tells us how an important part of nonverbal communication reading facial expressions can be. Listening to what a person says and ignoring what their face is telling you is getting only half of the story. There are instances when a person's words do not match their emotions, and their face betray what they are actually thinking and feeling. This is where the importance of knowing how to read facial expressions comes in.

Before we proceed to the techniques involved in reading facial expressions, you first need to be aware of what are referred to as universal emotions. There are facial expressions that are common to all cultures, and these are the following:

- Happiness
- Sadness
- Surprise
- Fear
- Disgust
- Anger
- Contempt

If you familiarize yourself with the facial expressions associated with these emotions, you will become good at identifying them in other people. But then there are facial expressions that do not remain for a long time. They're referred to as micro-expressions since they pass quickly and are almost imperceptible to the untrained observer.

34

READING THE EYES & THE EYEBROWS

THE EYES

The eyes are the first thing you focus on when looking at a person's face, especially in a conversation. They reveal much about what a person is thinking and feeling and is therefore referred to as "the windows to the soul." Someone even said that if you want to read someone's mind, you need only to look into their eyes. It may sound poetic, and indeed, you will often find this phrase mentioned in poetry or lyrics of songs. In fact, many artists have already capitalized on it.

It turns out that the eyes might indeed be the windows through which one can see another person's soul, or mind, or emotions, if you would. A growing number of studies shows that looking at a person's eyes may be a powerful way to gain special access to the human mind. And what's even more interesting is that even if people don't want you to find out what they actually think and feel, there is no way they can hide their thoughts and emotions through their eyes. People simply cannot change the behavior of their eyes.

EYE-BLOCKING

Blocking the eyes is often observed in people when they don't like what they see. A subtler way of covering the eyes comes in the form of excessive blinking, or sometimes, eye-rubbing. When you notice a person trying to shield their eyes, it could be a sign of disagreement or disbelief. Eye-blocking is a powerful nonverbal indication that a person dislikes something. And it's not something that's observed only in people who have normal vision. Even children who have been born blind cover their eyes as a natural response to hearing something they don't like.

PUPILLARY RESPONSE

Perhaps the most important observation to make in reading the eyes is the way the pupils respond. Changes in pupil size reflect how a person processes information and how relevant they perceive that information to be. When we are excited about something we see, the natural response of our pupils would be to increase in size. Pupil size also increase when we're processing information, such as trying to remember a phone number or a formula for a math problem, for instance.

Combine pupillary response with where a person is looking and it will give you an idea what people like or prefer. If you're presenting two options to someone, for instance, you will know which of the two they will prefer because they will fix their eyes on it. When they find it difficult to choose between two options, their eyes would switch back and forth between the two, but ultimately, their final gaze would be on the object they will end up choosing.

THE EYEBROWS

Eyebrows tell a lot about what an individual is feeling. Since they're near the eyes, they are highly visible. However, there's not a lot of muscles that control them, which limits what they try to convey. If you want to learn how to read a person's feelings through their eyebrows, you only need to check the direction their eyebrows are raised or lowered.

LOWERED EYEBROWS

Lowered eyebrows may indicate that a person is trying to hide something. It's designed to conceal the eyes, but only to a certain degree. When coupled with a lowered head, it could mean that the person may have a hidden desire or intention. In some cases, it could also mean annoyance or anger, perhaps saying something like, "I'm not pleased with you right now, and I don't want to look at you."

RAISED EYEBROWS

When the eyebrows are raised, on the other hand, it could indicate feelings of surprise or shock. This usually happens because of the eyes being opened wider, perhaps to allow the person to see better what the reason for the surprise is. Also, the greater the feeling of surprise, the higher the rise of the eyebrows are.

Aside from surprise, raised eyebrows could also mean that the person is asking for attention. In a class or any meeting, for instance, when the facilitator asks a question and raises their eyebrows, this indicates that they are inviting for someone to answer their question. Meanwhile, it could also indicate openness or submission. When a person raises their eyebrow, they may be saying, "You can look into my eyes and see that I can be trusted."

At the same time, raised eyebrows could mean that a person is attracted to you. On the other hand, when only one eyebrow is raised, it indicates that a person is cynical or suspicious. When you're sharing a message that might sound too good to be true to the other person, for instance, they could raise an eyebrow and say, "Are you sure?" or "Do you really know what you're talking about?"

READING MICROEXPRESSIONS

It's easy to read someone's expression when they're being genuine and authentic. There are facial expressions, though, that come out as a result of the person trying to conceal their true feelings. These are referred to as microexpressions. These facial expressions occur when the brain's emotion center appropriately responds to a stimulus, but the person tries to conceal their true emotion. Knowing how to read and interpret these expressions is an essential part of reading and analyzing people.

Earlier, we mentioned that there are seven universal expressions. These same expressions also make up microexpressions. Here's how to read each one of them:

SURPRISE

Surprise is a response experienced as a result of an unexpected event. It can have several valences, which means it can either be neutral, positive, or negative. When someone is surprised, they may either fight or flee depending on the level of intensity as a result of the stimuli. In a surprise microexpression, people will try to hide the fact that they are surprised by something. This is often accompanied by raised and curved eyebrows, producing horizontal wrinkles on the forehead. It also causes the eyelids to open, with the sclera or the white of the eye showing on all corners. The jaws are also open, exposing teeth that are parted, although there is no tension present that seems to stretch the mouth.

FEAR

Fear is a strong emotion induced by perceived threat or danger. When a person is afraid, they either want to flee, hide, or freeze. A fear microexpression, in particular, is evidenced by eyebrows that are raised and drawn together, as well as wrinkles in the center of the forehead between the brows. It's also marked with raised upper eyelids with only the upper part of the sclera showing. Meanwhile, it causes the mouth to open with the lips being slightly tensed and drawn back.

DISGUST

Most people won't let others know when they're feeling a strong disapproval or revulsion toward something they find offensive or unpleasant. However, if you know how to read a disgust microexpression, you'll know when you've offended someone and what necessary actions to take to make them feel better. It's not that difficult to know when a person is feeling disgusted and is trying to hide it because you will notice the upper eyelid raising. The lower lip will be raised, too, and the nose, wrinkled, when a person is disgusted with something. Finally, their cheeks will be raised, and lines will be visible below their eyes.

ANGER

Anger is an emotion that can't be easily hidden, and yet many people are really good at concealing their anger. When you have a hunch that a person is angry, you can confirm it by checking their facial expressions. In anger microexpression, the eyebrows are usually lowered and are drawn together. This expression causes vertical lines to appear between the brows. The eyes may also bulge and gazing really hard at the object of anger. The lips, on the other hand, are firmly pressed together, with the lower lip being tensed. Finally, the nostrils may be dilated and the jaw jutting out.

HAPPINESS

Genuine happiness is an expression that's difficult to hide. It's usually accompanied with a huge smile where the corners of the lips are fully drawn back and up. The mouth may not be fully parted, but the teeth are usually exposed. The cheeks, too, are raised, with wrinkles running from the outer part of the nose to the outer lip. The lower eyelids also show wrinkles, and crow's feet are present outside the eyes. A person who fakes happiness may show some of these expressions, but not all. For instance, with a fake expression of happiness, the muscles on the side of the eyes are usually not engaged, resulting in a suspicious look. Speaking of eyes, the eyes are the best reference when trying to find out if a person is faking happiness. Whenever you look at a smiling face, look at the eyes, as well, and see if the eyes are also "smiling." If the eyes aren't "smiling," there's a chance that the person is faking it.

SADNESS

Sadness is one expression we must all learn to identify, especially in a generation where depression is becoming more common. While sadness is one of the hardest expressions to fake, a lot of people are really good at it. To find out whether a person is trying to conceal sadness, look only in their eyes. Just as with other emotions, sadness is given away by the eyes. Moreover, sadness microexpression is also evidence by the eyebrows being drawn in and up, plus, by the triangulation of the skin below the eyebrows. The corner of the lips, too, are drawn down, with the lower lip pouting out.

CONTEMPT

Contempt is the most powerful microexpression, and it's also one of the easiest to detect since it's usually manifested with a smirk. However, there are times that contempt can be mistaken for happiness because of the half-smile that comes with it. It's far from happiness, though, if you know how to read the expression. In many cases, it's registered in terms of a slight smile that's asymmetrical. Contempt is actually not included in psychologist Paul Eckman's six basic emotions. To him, contempt is a mixture of anger and disgust. However, we include it on our list since like the six basic emotions, it's one that's commonly observed in people.

HOW TO ANALYZE PEOPLE BASED ON HOW THEY TALK

READING THROUGH PEOPLE'S WORDS

Words are very powerful. Not only do they convey what a person thinks or feels, but they also reflect the personality of the person speaking. Everything a person says reveals something about their personality. People's words are perfectly aligned with their thoughts and beliefs, and ultimately, their actions, in such a way that each of them reveal the same thing about them.

Even if it seems that a person's words carry no weight, they can say a great deal about a person's desires. They also say a lot about people's fears and insecurities.

Let's examine this statement:

"Hey, did you gain weight after that dinner last night?"

At first glance, it would seem that the statement is some kind of joke and has no other meaning, but if you examine it carefully, you will realize that it says a lot about the person who said it. The truth is that our perception of things is strongly compelled by the things we are most concerned about. In short, we only notice those things that we care about the most. Take a look at the statement once more. The first thing that person noticed was the weight of the person he was talking to. Perhaps he saw his friend wearing something that made her look bigger, but that could mean that he is also concerned about his own physical appearance and is suffering from low self-esteem.

Of course, our analysis isn't 100% accurate since there are several other factors that should be considered. Nevertheless, that was just one way you can find out more about people simply by analyzing their speech.

Let's look at another example.

You're in the playground watching your kids play with other children and one parent keeps telling his child to be careful. When you look carefully, there's really no reason for that parent to be too concerned about his child's safety since the playground was designed for safety. In reality, it's the person's perception that caused him to believe that the situation is more unsafe than it really was. It's safe to say that the person tends to worry a lot, and his perception exaggerates possible outcomes of certain situations, which in this case was the probability of his child getting hurt.

What do these scenarios tell us? They tell us that the way a person speaks reveals something about their insecurities and their deep needs, and that even if they had a different intention when they said what they said.

WORD CLUES

We often say that the eyes are the window to the soul, right? If that's the case, then the words are the portal to the mind. If you are to get to know people the closest that you can, listen only to the words they say and how they say them. You'll also get to know a person better by reading their writings. That's why there's an idea that every time you read a book, whether fiction or nonfiction, what you're actually doing is entering the mind of the author. Our words represent what's in our minds, and there are certain words we say that reflect our behavioral characteristics. These are referred to as word clues.

When analyzing people through their speech, identifying word clues help increase the chances of you finding out what their personality type is. Word clues are not a formula, though. On their own, they don't automatically let you read a person instantly and know what their personality traits are or what they're trying to say. However, they do help an observer make logical guesses on other people's behavioral characteristics. Here are ways word clues can provide you with insight into people's personality or behavioral characteristics when they talk.

I WAS ABLE TO VISIT THERE AGAIN.

The keyword in this statement is "again." In a sense, the speaker is saying that he was able to visit the particular place sometime before. The person is making sure that people will know that they were able to spend money to travel in the past. This kind of talk shows that the person speaking needs a boost of self-image. The same is true with the statement, "I got another promotion." The word clue here is "another," which conveys the message that the person received a previous promotion. It would seem that the speaker may need praise from others to reinforce their self-esteem.

I WORKED HARD FOR THIS.

The word "hard" here may suggest that the person speaking have a high standard or goals that are difficult for average people to achieve. Perhaps they may have achieved something more challenging than their usual goals. The word "hard" could also mean that the person values delayed gratification, or holds the belief that dedication and hard work results in good results. If you're working in the HR department and got the chance to interview an applicant who seem to have such characteristics, it would be a good idea to consider that applicant because their characteristics would make them a good employee since they would likely not shy away from difficult or challenging projects.

I DECIDED TO GO WITH THIS MODEL.

In the statement, the word clue "decided" implies that the person is one who thinks things through before making a decision. The person seems to be saying that he weighed various options prior to purchasing the item. By using the word "decided" the person speaking is saying that he is not impulsive. If he was, he could have just said, "I just bought it." In this case, the word "just" indicates that the person usually makes decisions without giving much thought about the purchase.

Just by word clue "decided," one can make a hypothesis that the person thinks before he acts, that he carefully weighs his options before making a decision. This should also give the idea that the person speaking is an introvert. If you're the listener, you should realize that introverts think before they speak. Knowing this is crucial if you are into business. Knowing whether a person is introvert or extrovert can give you a huge advantage when you're trying to sell them anything.

I DID WHAT WAS RIGHT.

The keyword "right" in this statement suggests that the person has a strong sense of right and wrong. Perhaps before making a decision, the person goes through a moral or ethical dilemma, but in the end was able to come up with a fair decision. By saying that he did what was right, the person is implying that he has enough strength of character that helped him make the right decision even in the midst of opposition.

DETECTING LIES THROUGH A PERSON'S SPEECH

It's not that difficult to detect when someone is lying to you, especially if you're already a parent. Parents are really good at finding out when their child is lying and is trying to hide something from them. However, there are people who are just good at not telling the truth. But no matter how good a liar is, psychological research suggests that these people always give off subtle clues that give them away. The only key, though, is that you know what to look for.

THEY CAN'T REMEMBER EXACT DETAILS

One way to spot a liar is by testing their accuracy with details. If a person is lying, they will make up stories on the spot. You will notice this easily because they will use the present tense instead of the past. And if you subtly ask them to tell the story in reverse order, there's very little chance they can do so. They will also hesitate at first since they still have to think about what they need to say and not get caught. When a person is lying, their brain will exert more effort, especially when they're trying to tell a story in reverse. Overtime, they will experience something called a 'cognitive workload'. This will make their brain work harder and they will eventually give themselves away.

THEY SEEM TO HAVE PREPARED ANSWERS

Sometimes, a person who is lying will have prepared answers to more obvious questions. They usually have a hunch that they're going to be interrogated, and this gives them a chance to prepare their answers. You'll easily catch when one is lying because they won't pause to remember details. They also give more details than is asked of them. And finally, they will volunteer certain information so as to appear that they are being honest, and then leave when the conversation seems to lead to them being challenged.

THEIR VOICE CHANGE

A change in the pitch of someone's tone can be a sign that the person is not telling you the truth. The pitch or tone of their voice will either rise or fall when they feel they are being suspected, and this is normal. They will also clear their throats more often as their vocal cords tighten and their saliva dries up. One of the reasons for this is nervousness. When a person who is lying begins to panic, their breathing will change from normal to rapid, and their heart rate and blood flow will increase, resulting in a change in voice. In some cases, they will deliberately change the tone or pitch of their voice to add emphasis to a particular word that will make them sound more believable.

THEY REPEAT A WORD OR PHRASE

The main priority of a person who is lying to make sure they convince you. One of the things they will do in order to achieve their goal is to repeat some words. It's their attempt not only to validate the lie in their minds but to buy them some time to gather their thoughts. When a person is lying, they may also use fillers in their sentences, such as begin a speech with 'actually' or 'well'. Again, this is a delaying tactic. People who are lying also focus on negation and will use a lot of words like 'no', 'did not', 'never', and 'not'. They will also use excluding words like 'but' and 'without' to appear more credible.

THEY FREQUENTLY PAUSE MID-SENTENCE

When people are lying, they usually make stories on the spot, causing them to think "on the fly." This requires a lot of effort from the brain, which we already discussed a little while ago. As a result, they will tend to pause frequently, sometimes even right in the middle of a sentence. A person speaking truthfully will seldom do this since the details they need to say come out naturally, and that they don't need a lot of effort to recollect an idea or a thought.

Sometimes, and as mentioned earlier, some liars would try to avoid pauses by preparing answers to obvious questions in advance. It would be difficult for them to provide details to more probing questions, though, so as the interrogation begins to go deeper, they will have a hard time coming up with answers and will begin to pause mid-sentence.

THEY PROVIDE TOO MUCH INFO

Providing information that's not requested is usually a sign that a person is not being truthful. This is a defense mechanism grounded on the idea that if they provide enough information, there's a higher chance that they will be believed on. It's also a tactic used to block interruptions. When asked one question, the person lying will usually talk fast and add unnecessary details to try to shut down the interrogator. Giving too much information is also an attempt to change the subject to direct the conversation away from the person. If the person you're interrogating gives you very long answers to simple questions, there's a huge chance that the person is hiding something.

THEY PRETEND THAT THEY ARE HONEST

Liars will do their best to make you believe they are sincere and honest. Once they feel they are being suspected, they will try to appear as honest as possible and use words like 'honestly'. They will also provide you with information that's true and even admit to minor offenses to prove their "honesty," although at the same time, they will do their best to deny major offenses. Sometimes, the liar will even try to pull off something dramatic like crying to appear really convincing.

They Get Defensive

This is the more obvious clue that a person is not telling the truth. They will deny that they are lying and even say something that will make you feel guilty. You might hear something like, "I would never do that," or "I would never lie to you." In some cases, the liar will become very angry if you keep on persisting, while at the same time flat out denying their offense. This is what separates a truthful person from one who is lying. A truthful person, when accused of something, will deny it, but will make sure they provide you enough information to convince you, but in a gentle way. A liar, on the other hand, will flat out deny and get defensive to try to put you off.

They Change The Subject

Imagine your partner spending the entire night out with friends. When asked, he tells you the truth, but then begins to narrate a highly detailed account of where they went and what they did. After a while, he talks about something else entirely. This is what it means for someone to change the subject, and its aim is to distract you. In other times, it would seem that there are important details omitted from the story. This, too, is a good sign that the person is not telling you the entire truth. They will also tend to contradict themselves, and their stories usually don't make sense. When you feel that a person is lying to you, continue asking pressing questions. Since the person is basically just manufacturing a story on the spot, they will have a lot of inconsistencies in their testimony along the way.

HOW TO ANALYZE PEOPLE IN A PROFESSIONAL SETTING

THE IMPORTANCE OF READING YOUR CO-WORKERS PERSONALITIES

Personality plays a major role in the workplace. When you understand how your personality affects other people and vice versa, you'll be able to make better choices and decisions at work. It also helps improve how you communicate not only with your colleagues but with your seniors.

One thing you need to understand, though, is that there's more to personalities than just a person being introverted or extroverted. Many times, this is where our focus lies when the subject of personalities is discussed. However, it's just one piece of the entire puzzle. Regardless of whether a person is introverted or extroverted, people will have varying degrees of intelligence, and this makes all the difference.

When it comes to reading people in the workplace, being able to recognize subtle differences in your co-worker's personalities will help you know each of them better. For instance, it will help you recognize which of your colleagues are the adventurous type and which ones are more conservative. Recognizing this helps you understand how to better work with people of varying personalities, since people's personalities will definitely affect the way they make decisions. Some people will be easy to invite to a drink after work, while others believe they should stay and work overtime.

Research shows that individuals who are able to better understand people's personalities tend to be happier in their place of work since they their understanding helps them respond appropriately to their colleagues. It's not only personalities that you need to learn how to read, though. In the workplace, you also need to be a master of reading body language cues if you are to help promote a healthier and more productive workplace.

READING BODY LANGUAGE IN THE OFFICE

Communication is key to productivity in the workplace. It helps everyone be on board and work as a team. When it comes to communication, however, we already know that words are only a part of it; body language is what communicates most of what a person thinks or feels. Being aware of cues helps you assess the message your colleagues are sending, as well as the message you are sending them.

IN SMALL GROUP SETTINGS

Observing the body language of a colleague or a subordinate can help you decide how to proceed during a meeting. In small group or one-on-one settings, for instance, paying attention to body language helps you recognize whether an employee is lacking in confidence, is having trouble with a project they're currently working on, or is being dishonest and trying to hide something from you or the company. By knowing how to read body language, you can determine who among the team needs additional training or coaching to enhance their self-confidence. It can also help you come up with ways to help an employee who is struggling with a task. And finally, it can help you uncover lies and deceit that may be detrimental to the organization.

DURING PRESENTATIONS OR MEETINGS

When presiding a meeting or giving a presentation, knowing how to gauge people's body language will help you determine how the audience perceive your message. When you notice your audience avoiding eye contact, for instance, it may be a sign that they are already bored. The same may be true when you employees fidgeting a lot with. On the other hand, if you notice an employee avoiding eye contact, crossing their arms, and seems to be turning away from your direction, there's a chance they're not 100% sold out on what you're saying. By understanding how body language works, you can make adjustments like make the meeting more interactive to keep your audience from getting bored. Or if you notice some who don't seem to agree with you, you can address them directly and open up the discussion with them to find out whether or not they want to suggest anything.

FIRST IMPRESSIONS COUNT

It's important to be aware of first impressions when meeting someone in the workplace for the first time. This is especially true when clients visit the office. By paying attention to non-verbal cues, you can maintain self-control and make sure that you can establish a positive tone in every meeting or interaction. It can also help you ascertain the tone of the meeting and even influence the outcome of your meetings. Study says it only takes an average of 7 seconds for someone to make a first impression. In most cases, body language plays a huge role in this. Your body language can either make or break transactions. In the same manner, the body language of your guest can help you decide how to approach the meeting.

EYE CONTACT IS IMPORTANT

We've found out in an earlier section that gazing at a person's lips is more effective in communication that gazing in their eyes. That doesn't mean that eye contact isn't as important, though. Whether at home, when dating, in coaching someone, in teaching a child, or in doing business, eye contact is no doubt one of the most essential communication tools. Nothing conveys sincerity and openness than looking straight at a person's eyes during conversation. Of course, we've learned that avoiding eye contact doesn't always mean the person is hiding something or isn't interested. However, maintaining eye contact is still very crucial, especially during first meetings. When a customer, supplier, or even a colleague doesn't seem to want to maintain eye contact, it could be that they're simply shy or perhaps being respectful. However, you still need to watch out because it could also mean that they're being evasive about something.

WATCH OUT FOR HAND GESTURES

Other than the eyes, the hands are the most expressive parts of the human body when it comes to communication. With proper use, the hands can greatly enhance communication, even non-verbal ones. When it comes to hand gestures, one of the main rules to keep in mind is that hands should be kept away from the face when talking. If you notice someone in the workplace placing their hands near their face like rubbing the cheek or the head, it's generally considered a sign of anxiety. In the same manner, when someone places their hand in a way that seems to cover the mouth or eyes, it signals that they may be lying or hiding something. As a rule, hand movements should be limited to emphasizing a point rather than unnecessary fidgeting.

PERSONAL SPACE

There's a branch of knowledge that deals with the amount of space people perceive as acceptable between themselves and others. It's called proxemics. According to this idea, the way humans use space affects their behavior and the behavior of the people around them. It also affects communication and social interaction. When meeting people for the first time, you will immediately find out what kind of personality they have just by observing how much space they give between themselves and other people in the room.

People who are comfortable with being as near as three feet can be considered very sociable, but also intimidating. When you notice a colleague always distancing themselves and never intentionally entering within 8 feet of another person's space, that colleague can be viewed as either shy or disinterested. The maximum acceptable social distance between oneself and another person, especially a stranger, is 4 feet. Of course, there will be times when invading personal space is acceptable, like when inside a crowded elevator or public transport. However, in the workplace, maintaining a distance of at least four feet from another person, especially one you're not too familiar with is what's considered as appropriate.

IDENTIFY MICROEXPRESSIONS

You're probably already aware of what microexpressions are since we've discussed the subject in an earlier section. These are fleeting and involuntary signs of what a person genuinely feels and are present whether a person is happy, excited, sad, angry, or indifferent. Microexpressions occur when an individual tries to conceal a feeling whether unconsciously or deliberately. When you catch someone displaying a microexpression on its peak, it can really give you a clear indication of what the person is feeling. Learn how to read microexpressions as it can be of great use when you're negotiating or trying to close a deal, for instance.

DON'T FORGET THE CONTEXT

Context is everything when it comes to reading body language. In the workplace, most especially, it's crucial that you are aware of the context that a person is believed to be communicating with body language. Situations in the workplace can be stressful most of the time, and people will display body language that could be taken out of context. For instance, a coworker who seems to be distancing himself from the rest of the team may not be doing it intentionally; it's probably just because he's zoning in on his task and doesn't want any distractions.

Before making conclusions, it's also important that you are aware of the baseline of a particular person. Familiarize yourself with each of your colleagues and even your seniors, and find out how they respond to situations under normal circumstances. That way, you'll immediately recognize whenever there are inconsistencies in their behavior as shown through their body language.

READING JOB APPLICANTS' BODY LANGUAGE

Having the ability to read body language is crucial when you're working in the HR department. Being able to interpret social cues can aid in your decision-making of whether to recommend an applicant for hiring or not. Most large organizations have people in the HR who have been trained to do just this. For small businesses, however, the art of interviewing is everything but easy.

One important thing interviewers should understand is that an applicant's cultural background is a very important thing to consider. Cultural influences how people think, and as much as possible, you would want to hire someone who would fit your company's cultures. Some companies, for instance, hire people who show nonverbal qualities that reinforce social extraversions and great self-confidence. On the other hand, organizations that value cooperation and innovation are attracted to applicants with more reserved qualities.

When interviewing applicants, be very observant of their body language to find out what kind of personality they carry. Identifying an applicant's qualities simply by interpreting their body language can give you an upper hand in the selection process. At the same time, you also need to realize that body language and nonverbal behavior can be different from country to country and culture to culture. Even in the United States, there are body language that are unique to one state. And while people from the West tend to be more outgoing, those from the eastern cultures tend to be more reserved and less direct with bodily gestures. An employer should be aware of this fact and not hold all candidates to one standard or expectation.

Nonverbal cues to consider when interviewing candidates include the following:

- Eye contact
- Facial expressions
- Voice modulation
- Handshake
- Verbal articulation
- Posture
- Hand gestures

Job interviews can be very stressful even for the most experienced candidate. For this reason, interviewers should understand that it's okay if applicants show some sign of nervousness. You will notice this at the start of the interview; hands are a bit shaky, eyes may be blinking a lot, arms are somewhat folded, and posture is stiff. These are normal, so it's okay to overlook them as long as you observe that the candidate begins to relax within 10 minutes to the interview.

It usually takes around this amount of time for candidates to warm up and feel more comfortable. Signs of confidence, such as a smile and improved eye contact will come out naturally when this happens. However, if a person's nonverbal cues and overall body language do not change or worsen as the interview progresses, it's questionable whether the candidate is socially inept. What's worse is that they may not be competent enough for the job they're applying for, which explains the lack of confidence.

Of course, it doesn't always mean that if a person shows negative body language, they're automatically socially awkward or incompetent. It could be that they just need a little help with their self-confidence. Nevertheless, applicants who are confident usually display some nonverbal cues that show their assertiveness. This includes regular eye contact, posture, and social skills.

At the end of the day, you don't want to consider body language alone when interviewing an applicant. Not everyone is going to be charismatic or sociable anyway, and that is not your aim. As an interviewer, the thing you should most attend to are the qualities that are important and relevant for the position.

HOW TO ANALYZE PEOPLE IN A ROMANTIC SETTING

BODY LANGUAGE SIGNS TO LOOK OUT FOR ON FIRST DATE

Many things in this world are full of mystery, among which are first dates. Such occasions are often accompanied with mixed messages. The good news is reading the body language of the person you're dating is possible, and it can help you big time. The human brain is wired in such a way that you immediately know whether someone is physically attractive or not, at least in the beholder's own eyes. We simply recognize within seconds if we like someone or not, and when we do, we communicate our attraction with either verbal or nonverbal cues. That said, here are the things to be aware of the next time you go out with a prospective partner for a romantic dinner.

LEANING IN

We all want to get closer to people we are attracted to. It's just as natural as metals are attracted to magnets. If you notice your date continuously leaning in toward do, there's a good chance they're interested and telling you through their body language. This is especially true when you're in a group. Even on a non-romantic setting, people in a group tend to lean towards someone, like the leader of the group, because they want to show that they are interested in what the person is saying. On the other hand, if your date tends to pull back every time you approach, it may be a sign that they find you unattractive or uninteresting.

STEADY EYE CONTACT

We've discussed several times how important eye contact is when it comes to body language. When you're out on a date, one way to find out if your date likes you or not is by considering the intensity of their gaze and the degree of eye contact they make with you. Prolonged eye contact simply means interest. On the other hand, it could also spark interest. Psychologist Arthur Aron did a study on the science of love. He came up with 36 questions that according to him can break down emotional barriers and lead to friendship or romance.[6] As part of the study, he had six couples stare silently at each other's eyes for about four minutes. The experiment generated such connection that one of the couples ended up marrying each other.

---

[6] https://www.nytimes.com/2015/01/11/fashion/no-37-big-wedding-or-small.html

It goes without saying that a steady gaze from your date is a good sign, unless they're staring in such a way that sends creep down your spine. You also need to observe the pupils. Dilated pupils means the person is excited to see you and can't take their eyes off of you (Yes, just like in the song). On the other hand, if you notice the pupils shrink, it means they're not liking what they're seeing in front of them.

BLOCKING

Blocking is the opposite of leaning in. When a person seems to position away from you or use body language intended to block you off, don't expect that person to like you in any way. Blocking is a type of "distancing body language." People show this gesture when they're not comfortable with the person they are with. When we want to be with someone, we tend to face them directly with square shoulders and feet, but do the opposite if we're not interested. Signs you need to look out for are crossed arms, crossed leg with knees up, and elbows on the table creating a barrier with the arms.

DIRECTION OF THE TOES

The direction of a person's toes is a good indicator of whether or not they are interested in you. When on a date, check to see whether your date's feet are pointing in your direction. If they are, then that's a good sign, because it means your date is interested in getting to know you more. If the toes are pointing away from you, particularly toward the door, that's bad news because it's a good indicator that your date is not that into you and may be thinking of other things instead. It's the same thing with crossing legs. Legs that are crossed may be a sign that your date wants to leave ASAP, but not unless the legs are crossed toward you. If they are, then that's definitely good news.

STUMBLING OVER WORDS

Even the most intelligent individuals trip over their words when they are around the person they like. If you're date is experiencing the same, cut them some slack because it only means they're anxious, and that means they are interested in you. Strong attractions can affect not only the voice[7] but speech in general. Attraction does a lot of things to the human body, particularly the brain. For one, it causes the brain to release hormones that increases blood flow, making the heart race and the palms sweat. This can sometimes lead to anxiety, which in turn results in slurred speech.[8]

Men, in general, get easily tongue-tied when talking to women they are attracted to. The reason is simple: they have a lot of pressure on them. What kind of pressure? The pressure to appear pleasant to the opposite sex. This pressure can lead

---

[7] https://www.abc.net.au/news/2017-09-25/voice-changes-reveal-love-attraction/8974012

[8] https://www.calmclinic.com/anxiety/symptoms/slurred-speech

to stress and anxiety, and we know that these two can lead men to do silly things, one of which is getting tongue-tied.

USING BODY LANGUAGE TO ENHANCE YOUR RELATIONSHIP

If there is one area in your life that will greatly benefit from your knowledge of reading body language, it's your relationship. Body language impacts any relationships more than words. Aside from simply knowing how to read body language, however, it also makes sense to also know how to use them to improve your relationship. Here's how:

MIRROR-MIRROR

So much of your relationship with your partner happens on a subconscious level. It's the things you do that can't be put into words. It's whenever you feel like you can read your partner's mind and vice versa, or when you complete each other's sentences, or when you walk, talk, and act in very similar ways. Studies say that this is a sign of deep connection between two people. [9] It's called mirroring.

Mirroring can teach us a lot about our romantic relationships. In most long-term relationships, this practice isn't as active, although it does happen naturally. For instance, if you're holding hands with

---

[9] https://www.ncbi.nlm.nih.gov/pmc/articles/PMC3840169/

your partner while walking, it means the two of you are in tune with one another, and this causes a production of "love chemicals" in the brain, giving you a boost of good feelings that make the both of you feel closer to each other.

Early on in your relationship, mirroring can help you get to know each other more. As your relationship strengthens, it becomes more organic. There will be times you will notice it's not happening as it should. For instance, if you and your partner used to hold hands while walking -- both in tune to each other's gait -- and now one of you walks ahead most of the time, it could be a sign that there's something off in your relationship.

Take this as an opportunity for you to evaluate your relationship. Talk to your partner, too, and if your partner also feels the disconnect, then the two of you can work to rebuild lost rapport.

THE POWER OF A TOUCH

Touch is a fundamental need of humans. It comes before sight and speech and is the first and last language that we speak. Among adults, touch communicates many things, including love, gratitude, compassion, and tenderness. It can also communicate fear and anger.

In our relationships, especially romantic ones, touch helps us feel more connected with our loved ones. The reason is that touch releases what is called the "love hormone." It also lowers blood pressure and reduces stress. And these results are true whether you're the one being hugged or the one giving it. That said, touch is a key factor to a lasting romantic relationship. It even outranks sex. The reason is that while both a person's need for sex and the ability to practice it wanes over time, the need for touch and the ability to give it doesn't.

If you and your partner do not lack in this area and regularly hug each other, hold each other's hands, give massages, and cuddle, then your relationship is in good shape. On the other hand, if you notice your partner not touching you the way they used to, go talk to your partner why that is so. Most of the time, your partner isn't aware of it, especially if the reason for the lack of touch is your busy schedules at work and home.

The good news is you can always light the fire of romance again by intentionally using physical touch. When your partner comes home, for instance, hug him immediately. Also, try to bring back the holding-hands-while-walking thing you used to do when you were just starting. Talk to your partner about it, too. Tell him what you've observed about your relationship. If he wants to rebuild your relationship, he, too, will commit to be more intentional when it comes to giving physical touch.

ENTHUSIASTIC KISS

Kissing symbolizes a romantic relationship that is flourishing. For those who are still in the search for a potential partner, kissing helps in finding the right person. This is according to a study by Oxford University, which also found that kissing helps in getting a partner stay in a relationship.[10] And when you're in a relationship, kissing, in a sense, helps you read what's in your partner's mind. A soft kiss that lingers an extra second, for instance, means that your partner is happy to be with you and wishes to spend more time with you. This is especially true if other parts of the body are into the act; a warm kiss is usually partnered with a hug, in such a way that the hearts are pressed together.

Meanwhile, a kiss that's hard with closed lips means that your partner is trying to avoid intimacy. It could mean that there's tension between you or

---

[10] http://www.ox.ac.uk/news/2013-10-11-kissing-helps-us-find-right-partner-%E2%80%93-and-keep-them

that your partner has something against you. The same is true with hugging. If you're hugging with your bodies separated, it's a sign that you're treating it as an obligation. One way to fix this is to make a conscious effort to kiss and hug your partner with enthusiasm, followed with a loving gaze.

ADVANCED STRATEGIES FOR ANALYZING PEOPLE: COLD READING

Cold reading is a technique that allows one to analyze and interpret another person's intentions simply by observing nonverbal signals they give. It's a fundamental skill required of aspiring mentalists. Most of what we've been discussing so far is actually cold reading, although not on the 'mentalist' level. Being able to cold read people or decipher people's nonverbal behavior allows one to make judgments regarding the person's behavior and adjust one's behavior in accordance to the way the other person acts.

FEET NONVERBALS

We've already discussed how observing the direction of the feet can give us an idea what another person thinks. Most people do not realize, though, that feet nonverbals are the most accurate in reflecting what's inside another person's mind. The reason is that the feet, along with the legs, are the primary means of reaction for human beings when it comes to environmental threats. It's embedded in our limbic brain that whenever we are in situation where our wellbeing is threatened, the part of the body to always react first are the feet.

The feet are the component of the human body that initiates our fight or flight response by helping us either run out of danger or kick to fight back when there's no other alternative. For this particular reason, it's good to start from bottom to top when observing people instead of top to bottom. You'll be amazed at how honest the feet and legs are in the message they convey. That said, feet direction and the way the legs are crossed are two of the most important feet nonverbals you need to look out for.

FEET DIRECTION

It's very easy to predict what a person is thinking simply by observing the direction of their feet. The reason is that it is a natural tendency for us to turn toward people or things that we find interesting. This is an automatic response, and it can help us determine whether somebody is happy to see us or not. The next time you find yourself interacting with a friend or colleague, or even a stranger, for instance, try to pay attention to their feet.

If the other person is turning their feet slightly away from you or is repeatedly moving one foot outward, you can be sure that they want to be anywhere but with you. On the other hand, since people normally speak toe to toe, you will know if a person likes having a conversation with you if both their toes are pointed toward you as you speak.

CROSSED LEGS

Oftentimes, we cross our legs when we feel comfortable sitting down. We also cross our legs when we feel confident about ourselves. On the other hand, we never cross our legs when we're in a situation we're not comfortable to be in. And it's interesting to note that this behavior is influenced by our limbic brain. This part of the brain prioritizes our safety, which why we cross our legs whenever we feel safe and comfortable.

Just like feet direction, crossed legs reveal a lot about a person's intention. When two individuals are sitting side by side, for instance, the direction of their legs while crossed is very important. If the two are in good terms with each other, the leg that's on top will point toward the direction of the other person. On the other hand, if the two are not in good terms, or if one doesn't agree with the other person, they will shift their leg position so that the thigh block is blocking the other person.

Again, this action is a result of the limbic brain telling the body to protect itself.

TORSO NONVERBALS

The torso or the trunk of the body is where most of our significant organs such as the stomach, liver, lungs, and heart are housed. For that reason, it makes a lot of sense that the limbic part of the brain will automatically try to protect this are when it feels the body is being threatened, and that whether the danger is real or perceived. And that is the primary way you can read torso nonverbals.

One of the first reactions of the torso when danger is perceived is to lean back. This is the brain's way of telling the rest of the body to distance itself from the threat. This is the reason your reaction when something is thrown at you is to shift your upper body to try to avoid the object. In the same manner, when you're sitting or standing next to a person you don't like, your body's first reaction is lean away. The next time you see two people having a conversation, observe how their torsos are positioned. If both are sitting or standing near each other with shoulders squared, they definitely have connection.

Another way you can read someone's intentions by looking at their torso is by observing how they shield their upper body. Shielding the torso is an automatic response to perceived danger. When people try to shield their torso, it's almost certainly because they are not comfortable with the situation they are in. Men, will do this in subtle ways, so as not to appear fearful or weak. They often do this by fixing their tie knot, adjust their shirt sleeve, or play with their watch or any accessory near their chest. When you see a man doing this, it's probably because he's uneasy and is unconsciously trying to protect himself.

Women are different and are often conspicuous in the way they attempt to safeguard themselves. In order to feel more secure in an uncomfortable situation, women usually cross their arms over their stomach.

ARMS NONVERBALS

The arms are often ignored when it comes to reading and interpreting nonverbal behavior. When we try to read people, we often focus on their facial expressions. We also sometimes observe the hands, but never the arms. However, the arms, too, can reveal a lot of information about a person.

The regal stance is one of the gestures we often do with our arms. It's when we place both our arms behind our back with our upper body either leaning a little bit forward or backward. Regardless of the direction of the body, the regal stance usually conveys that the person is attempting to distance themselves from something; the forward lean means that while the person is trying to keep distance, they are still a bit curious of the object they perceive as a threat.

Take a friend who comes to visit to see your newborn, for instance. Your child needs a diaper change and you invite your friend to continue the conversation while you're changing your baby's spoiled diaper. Since we tend to distance our arms and hands from things we don't like, your friend will most likely do the regal stance while watching you clean your newborn. When you observe someone doing the regal stance, it is almost always because they are experiencing unease.

Aside from protection, the arms are also used to mark territories. Humans may be social creatures, but they are territorial at the same time. That's why we feel a bit of uneasiness whenever we spend too much time with a person, and that is a result of our territorial nature. Arms on the waist is arguably the most common nonverbal projection of this nature of ours. When you see a person with their hands on the waist, it's either they are trying to establish control over their territory or trying to convey that they have an issue with another person.

HANDS AND FINGERS NONVERBALS

Nothing in this world is as unique as human hands. They can grasp, poke, pinch, hold, and even mold. Most importantly, the hands can be used to express one's self. When you're angry, you clench your first. When you're giving directions, you point with your finger. When you're trying to make a point, you wave your hands. It's also because of this power of our hands to express that it makes it easy for this part of the body to betray our intentions.

The hands reflect many subtle nuances in a person's behavior. They are used extensively to enhance a person's persuasiveness and credibility. In fact, when used correctly, hand gestures can significantly enhance the quality of a message, as well as its delivery.

The two most common hands and fingers nonverbals are hand steepling and thumb display. With hand steepling, all fingers of both hands touch to form a triangle, but without the palms touching. When a person does this, it means they are confident with their position and ideas. Aside from adding power to the delivery of a message, it also attracts people's attention.

Thumb display, too, is a powerful indicator of a person's confidence. If your hands are on your pocket but your thumbs are out, you are display confidence, albeit subconsciously. On the other hand, you may be experiencing something negative like stress or anxiety when you hide your thumbs inside your pockets or even clench them inside your palms.

FINAL THOUGHTS: CAN YOU REALLY FAKE BODY LANGUAGE?

While you can read a lot from other people's body language, you can learn from your own body language, as well. The nonverbal signals you display have a great impact on you. The question, however, is whether you can actually fake it 'til you make it? Well, the answer is both yes and no. There are nonverbals that can be learned through conscious thought and effort. Take the expressive use of hand gestures to convey honesty, for instance, or the keeping away of hands from the face to show confidence. These gestures can be learned over time.

And then there's the study by Amy Cuddy who popularized the idea that faking body language can help reduce stress and make you more confident. According to her research, confidence can be learned, and one way to learn it is by adopting poses that display optimism and assertiveness. Also known as power poses, these postures allow you to take up more space, and this has both physiological and psychological effects, causing you to feel more confident to take risks.

But then there are body language that cannot be faked. Microexpressions are an example of these. As we've already learned, these expressions come in the form of smiles, frowns, smirks, and wrinkles that though fleeting, can offer accurate windows into a person's thoughts and emotions. And one reason you can't fake microexpressions is that you cannot control the muscles involved in creating them. Of course, there are good poker players who have mastered the suppressing of these emotions, but when you observe them longer and more closely, they will eventually show signs that they are concealing something.

That said, studying how to read and analyze people through their body language is worth it. And this is a skill that shouldn't be taken for granted. When you know how to read people, you know what makes them comfortable or uncomfortable, and that allows you to make the right decisions when it comes to communicating or negotiating with them. Most importantly, learning about body language and reading people helps you change negative aspects of yourself and portray yourself to others in a more positive way.

-END-

Made in the USA
Middletown, DE
04 November 2019

77927822R00053